CHRIS CARROLL

Legendary Basketball Trivia

Greatest Ballers, Moments, and Records

First edition

This book was professionally typeset on Reedsy.
Find out more at reedsy.com

Contents

Introduction

Ever wondered who laced up their sneakers and stepped onto the hardwood with a dream that would change the game forever? Or maybe you're curious about the record-breaking moments that have fans leaping from their seats, spilling popcorn in excitement.

Right now, you're holding not just a book, but a courtside pass to the most thrilling performances basketball has to offer. This isn't just any sport; it's a realm where legends are made, where every dribble, dunk, and decisive moment captures the essence of human endeavor and spirit.

Who is this book for? If you've ever found yourself arguing over the greatest player of all time, digging through stats like a treasure hunter, or simply basking in the glow of a game well played, you're in the right place. From the casual fan who catches a game now and then, to the trivia buffs who sweat stats, and even the coaches and players themselves - this is your playbook.

As we dribble through the chapters, we'll uncover the stories that make this game more than just points on a scoreboard. It's about heart, history, and those hair-raising moments of human achievement.

So, lace up your sneakers, and let's take a leap into the legendary.

Because, in basketball, every second on the clock is a chance for magic. And who knows? By the end of this, you might just see the game with new eyes, ready to spot the next big moment - or make it yourself.

The Evolution of Basketball

Basketball: a game that has transcended its humble beginnings to become a global phenomenon. It's more than just a sport; it's a panorama of history, innovation, and spirit. Let's delve into the rich history and captivating details that have shaped basketball into what it is today.

The Invention of Basketball

1. James Naismith invented basketball in 1891 as a way to keep his students active during the cold winter months.
2. The first game was played with a soccer ball and two peach baskets as goals.
3. Naismith's original rules consisted of 13 basic rules that laid the foundation for the game.
4. The first public basketball game was played in Springfield, Massachusetts, in March 1892.
5. Basketball was initially intended as a non-contact sport; early players were penalized for running with the ball.
6. The first professional basketball game was played in 1898, seven years after the sport was invented.
7. Women's basketball began in 1892, just one year after the men's

game was invented, with Senda Berenson adapting Naismith's rules for women.

8. The first basketball was manufactured in 1894 by the A.G. Spalding Company.

9. The original peach baskets were replaced with metal hoops, nets, and backboards in 1906 because retrieving the ball from the baskets slowed down play.

10. Basketball became an Olympic sport in 1936 at the Berlin Olympics, and the medals were awarded by James Naismith.

Evolution of the Game

1. The NBA was founded on June 6, 1946, as the Basketball Association of America (BAA) before merging with the National Basketball League (NBL) in 1949 to become the NBA.

2. The original BAA consisted of 11 teams.

3. The first slam dunk was credited to Joe Fortenberry in 1936, while playing for the McPherson Globe Refiners at Madison Square Garden.

4. The shot clock was introduced in 1954 to increase the pace of the game and prevent teams from stalling. It was invented by Danny Biasone, the owner of the Syracuse Nationals.

5. The three-point line was not part of the original game; it was first introduced in a professional league by the American Basketball League (ABL) in 1961, brought fans out of their seats in the American Basketball Association (ABA) in 1967, and adopted by the NBA in 1979.

6. The NBA introduced the "Larry O'Brien Championship Trophy" in 1977, named after the former NBA commissioner.

7. The league introduced a salary cap for the first time in the 1984-1985 season to ensure competitive balance. They were the first professional sports league in the United States to implement salary caps.
8. The league's adoption of the no-charge zone under the basket was implemented in the 1997-1998 season to enhance player safety.
9. The WNBA was founded on April 24, 1996, and the first season was played in 1997.
10. The NBA implemented a concussion protocol in 2011 to address head injuries more effectively.
11. The introduction of sleeved jerseys in 2013 marked a significant departure from traditional tank-top basketball uniforms, but quickly returned to the traditional style in 2017.
12. The NBA implemented the coach's challenge rule in the 2019-2020 season.
13. The league has seen several changes in basketball design, the most recent being in 2021 when it switched back to Wilson as its official game ball manufacturer.

Historical Milestones

1. The NBA's first official game was played in Toronto between the New York Knickerbockers and the Toronto Huskies on November 1, 1946.
2. The longest game in NBA history lasted 78 minutes and was played between the Indianapolis Olympians and the Rochester Royals (now the Sacramento Kings) on January 6, 1951.
3. The first NBA game was broadcast on national television in 1953.
4. The NBA awarded its first Most Valuable Player (MVP) accolade in

1956, with Bob Pettit of the St. Louis Hawks honored as its inaugural recipient.

5. The NBA's inaugural international showcase took place in Tel Aviv, Israel, with an exhibition match marking the league's first venture overseas. Since then, it has expanded its global footprint by hosting exhibition games in a multitude of countries worldwide.

6. The Defensive Player of the Year Award was introduced in the 1982–1983 season.

7. The Sixth Man of the Year Award, honoring the best player coming off the bench, was introduced in the 1982–1983 season. Bobby Jones, a 76ers power forward, was the first recipient of the award in 1983.

8. The NBA's first Slam Dunk Contest was held in 1984 during the All-Star Weekend. Larry Nance, a forward for the Phoenix Suns, defeated Julius Erving, in the final round.

9. In 1990, Tokyo, Japan, hosted a groundbreaking event as the Phoenix Suns and Utah Jazz competed in the first NBA regular season game ever held outside of North America.

10. The NBA introduced the draft lottery system in 1985 to prevent teams from losing games intentionally to secure the top draft pick. This was implemented by commissioner David Stern.

11. The league's first-ever three-point contest was held during the All-Star Weekend in 1986.

12. The NBA's 50th anniversary was celebrated in 1996, commemorating half a century of basketball excellence.

13. In 2001, the NBA launched the National Basketball Development League (NBDL) or NBA D-League to develop young talent. It was renamed NBA G League after Gatorade became the title sponsor in the 2017–2018 season.

Technological Innovations and Social Impact

1. In 1999, The NBA became the first major sports league to create its own cable television network, NBA TV (originally named nba.com TV)

2. The NBA was the first league to broadcast a game in VR (virtual reality) in 2015, showcasing the league's innovative approach to fan engagement.

3. The NBA 2K eLeague, a professional eSports league, was launched in 2018, marking the league's expansion into competitive gaming. The NBA is the first US professional sports league to operate an eSports league.

4. In 2020, the NBA season was suspended for the first time in history due to the COVID-19 pandemic.

5. For the 2020-2021 season, the league unveiled a play-in tournament to decide the final playoff positions, aiming to heighten excitement and engagement among both teams and fans in the playoff chase.

6. In 2016, the NBA moved the All-Star Game from Charlotte due to a controversial law passed in North Carolina, showing the league's stance on social issues.

7. In 2020, the NBA established the Social Justice Coalition, dedicated to advancing a wide array of actions and initiatives aimed at championing social justice.

8. Advanced stats and player tracking technology were introduced in all NBA arenas to enhance analytics.

9. The NBA has been a leader in adopting social media, engaging fans worldwide through various platforms.

Expansion and Globalization

1. Basketball became an Olympic sport in 1936, and the United States won the first gold medal.
2. The first FIBA Basketball World Cup was held in Argentina in 1950. It was the first men's national team basketball tournament.
3. The 1992 United States men's Olympic basketball team, known as the "Dream Team", was the first American Olympic team to feature active NBA players.
4. The league's first international office was opened in Hong Kong in 1992
5. The first non-American to win the NBA MVP was Hakeem Olajuwon from Nigeria, in 1994.
6. The NBA's first expansion outside the United States occurred in 1995 with the addition of the Toronto Raptors and the Vancouver Grizzlies. The Grizzlies moved to Memphis in 2001.
7. The NBA's Basketball Without Borders program was launched in 2001 to promote the sport globally.
8. Yao Ming's entry into the NBA in 2002 significantly increased the league's popularity in China.
9. The NBA Academy program was introduced in 2016 to develop elite basketball prospects from outside the United States.
10. In 2019, The Toronto Raptors became the first team based outside of the United States team to win the NBA Championship.
11. The NBA launched the Basketball Africa League (BAL) in 2021, its first collaboration to operate a league outside North America.
12. As of 2023, a record 125 international players from about 40 countries and territories were represented in the NBA.
13. NBA games are broadcast in 214 countries and territories in more than 50 languages.

Memorable Achievements and Highlights

1. Team USA men's basketball team made their first Olympic appearance in 1936 in Berlin, Germany, capturing the gold medal.

2. Team USA men's basketball went unbeaten in Olympic play from 1936 to 1972, a streak ended controversially in the gold medal game against the Soviet Union in Munich.

3. The NBA's first Christmas Day games were played in 1947, starting a long-standing tradition.

4. Wilt Chamberlain scored 100 points in a single NBA game on March 2, 1962, the only player ever to do so in the NBA.

5. The Team USA women's basketball debuted in the 1976 Montreal Olympics, securing a silver medal in their first appearance.

6. The 1992 Barcelona Olympics saw the debut of the "Dream Team," the first American Olympic team to feature active NBA players, including Michael Jordan, Magic Johnson, and Larry Bird. They won the gold without ever calling a timeout.

7. On December 13, 1983, the Detroit Pistons set an NBA record by scoring 186 points in a single game, the highest by any team, during a triple-overtime victory against the Denver Nuggets with a final score of 186–184. This historic game saw a combined total of 370 points, making it one of the highest-scoring games in NBA history, with the Nuggets' 184 points ranking as the second-highest single-game team total.

8. The 1996 Olympics Team USA women's basketball, featuring Lisa Leslie, Sheryl Swoopes, and Rebecca Lobo, started a streak of consecutive gold medals that continued into 2024.

9. In 2008, The Phoenix Suns and the Denver Nuggets participated in the league's first outdoor game in the modern era at the Indian Wells Tennis Garden.

10. The largest attendance at any NBA event was recorded in 2010

during the All-Star Game at Cowboys Stadium in Arlington, Texas with 108,713 fans in attendance.

11. The record for the highest attendance at an NBA regular season game was set on January 13, 2023, when 68,323 spectators filled the Alamodome in San Antonio, Texas, USA, to see the Golden State Warriors triumph over the San Antonio Spurs with a score of 144-113.

12. Phil Jackson holds the record for the most NBA championships as a head coach, with 11 titles - six with the Chicago Bulls and five with the Los Angeles Lakers. He also has two titles as a player with the New York Knicks, bringing his total to 13 NBA championships - the most of all time.

13. The league has seen a quadruple-double only four times in its history, a testament to the rarity of the achievement.

- Nate Thurmond in 1974: 22 points, 14 rebounds, 13 assists, and 12 blocks
- Alvin Robertson in 1986: 20 points, 11 rebounds, 10 assists, and 10 steals
- Hakeem Olajuwon in 1990: 18 points, 16 rebounds, 11 blocks, and 10 assists
- David Robinson in 1994: 34 points, 10 rebounds, 10 assists, and 10 blocks

Iconic NBA Players

This collection showcases the incredible diversity, talent, and accomplishments of NBA players since the league's inception, offering a broad view of the individual achievements that have contributed to the rich history of the NBA.

1. The first player to be officially drafted in the NBA was Clifton McNeely in 1947. However, instead of embarking on a professional basketball career, he chose to follow a path in coaching, taking up a position at Pampa High School in Texas.
2. Michael Jordan retired from basketball three times before finally ending his career.
3. Kareem Abdul-Jabbar retired in 1989 with the most career points (38,387) in NBA history, a record he held until Lebron James surpassed him in 2023.
4. In 1962, Wilt Chamberlain set the single-game scoring record with 100 points.
5. Bill Russell won 11 NBA championships, the most by any player. The last 2 of his championship rings were won as a Head Coach/Player for the Boston Celtics.
6. During the 1961-62 season, Robertson achieved a historic milestone as the first NBA player to average a triple-double throughout

the entire season, recording 30.8 points, 12.5 rebounds, and 11.4 assists.

7. The shortest player in NBA history, Muggsy Bogues, stood at 5'3", while the tallest, Gheorghe Muresan and Manute Bol, were both 7'7".

8. Magic Johnson was the first rookie to win the NBA Finals MVP, achieving this in 1980.

9. Larry Bird and Magic Johnson's rivalry began in college and transitioned into their NBA careers, significantly boosting the league's popularity.

10. Michael Jordan won six NBA championships and five Finals MVP awards with the Chicago Bulls in the 1990s.

11. Shaquille O'Neal, recognized as one of the NBA's most dominant centers, boasts four NBA Championships (three with the Los Angeles Lakers and one with the Miami Heat) along with an Olympic Gold Medal.

12. Tim Duncan, known as "The Big Fundamental," won five NBA championships with the San Antonio Spurs.

13. Allen Iverson, at approximately 6 feet tall, was one of the smallest players to be named NBA MVP (2001).

14. Kobe Bryant scored 81 points in a single game in 2006, the second-highest total in NBA history.

15. In 2018, at 33 years and 24 days old, LeBron James set a record as the youngest player to achieve 30,000 career points.

16. Dirk Nowitzki is celebrated as one of the top shooting big men in basketball history. His tenure with the Dallas Mavericks spanned an unprecedented 21 seasons, the longest with a single franchise. His leadership in 2011 earned him the Finals MVP as he led Dallas to its first NBA championship.

17. Steve Nash clinched consecutive NBA Most Valuable Player (MVP) awards in 2005 and 2006, sparking debate with his first win over

Shaquille O'Neal, which challenged the conventional criteria for the league's MVP. The controversy continued into 2006 when Nash secured the MVP title once more, narrowly surpassing LeBron James and Kobe Bryant, further fueling discussions around the award's qualifications.

18. In 1995, Kevin Garnett was one of the first players to make a successful jump from high school to the NBA, paving the way for others.

19. In 2007, Dirk Nowitzki from Germany was the first European born player to win the NBA MVP.

20. Stephen Curry became synonymous with the three-point revolution, changing how the game is played. He currently holds the record for the highest number of career three-pointers, amassing a total of 3,680 threes which is increasing every game.

21. Russell Westbrook averaged a triple-double for three consecutive seasons, starting in 2016-2017.

22. Giannis Antetokounmpo won back-to-back MVP awards in 2019 and 2020, known for his versatility and dominance on both ends of the floor. He joins Kareem Abdul-Jabbar and LeBron James as the only players to win two MVPs before turning 26.

23. Hakeem Olajuwon is the only player in NBA history to win the MVP, Defensive Player of the Year, and Finals MVP in the same season (1994).

24. Starting in 2010, Kevin Durant won four scoring titles in five years, while playing with the Oklahoma City Thunder.

25. Chris Paul led the NBA in assists per game five times and steals per game six times.

26. Ray Allen retired holding the record for the most career three-point field goals made. He held that record until he was surpassed by Stephen Curry in 2021.

27. Jason Kidd retired ranked second all-time in both assists (12,091)

and steals (2,684) in NBA history.

28. Kawhi Leonard won the Finals MVP with two different teams, the San Antonio Spurs and Toronto Raptors, becoming the first player to win the award with a team from each conference.

29. Vince Carter is the only player in NBA history to have a career spanning 22 seasons.

30. Karl Malone and John Stockton are recognized as one of the most formidable NBA pairings never to secure a championship. Over their 18 seasons together with the Utah Jazz, they became synonymous with their exceptional pick-and-roll technique. Accumulating nearly 1,000 victories as a duo, they reached the NBA Finals on two occasions.

31. Despite being one of the greatest centers of his time, Patrick Ewing never won an NBA championship.

32. In his first season with the Suns, Charles Barkley won the MVP award while leading the team to a 62–20 record and a spot in the 1993 NBA Finals. The Suns lost to Michael Jordan's Bulls that year, and Barkley He never secured an NBA championship

33. John Stockton holds the record for the most career assists (15,806) and steals (3,265). In 17 of his 19 seasons in the NBA, he did not miss a single game.

34. Reggie Miller was known for his precise three-point shooting and clutch performances in the playoffs. Miller is a five-time NBA All-Star and ranks in the all-time fourth all-time in NBA three-pointers made.

35. Dwyane Wade led the Miami Heat to their first NBA championship in 2006 and won a total of three during his career.

36. Paul Pierce was nicknamed "The Truth" by Shaquille O'Neal and won an NBA championship with the Boston Celtics in 2008.

37. Carmelo Anthony is one of the top scorers in NBA history, but has never reached the NBA Finals.

38. David Robinson and Tim Duncan were nicknamed "The Twin Towers" and led the San Antonio Spurs to two NBA championships together.

39. Derrick Rose was the youngest player to win the MVP award at age 22.

40. Kyrie Irving's clutch three-pointer in Game 7 of the 2016 NBA Finals helped secure the Cleveland Cavaliers' first championship.

41. Damian "Dame Time" Lillard is known for his range and clutch shooting, having multiple game-winning buzzer-beaters.

42. Luka Dončić won the Rookie of the Year award in 2019 and has been compared to some of the NBA's greatest players due to his versatility and skill.

43. Trae Young is known for his deep three-point shooting and play-making skills.

44. Anthony Davis has been selected to four All-NBA First Teams and is known for his defensive prowess and scoring ability.

45. Jimmy Butler is known for his work ethic and defensive ability, leading the Miami Heat to the NBA Finals in 2020 and 2023.

46. Draymond Green, a four-time NBA champion, is a key player for the Golden State Warriors, is known for his versatility, defense, and playmaking.

47. Nikola Jokić, led the Denver Nuggets to their first NBA championship in franchise history. His outstanding performance earned him the first Bill Russell Finals MVP award.

48. Joel Embiid, a dominant center for the Philadelphia 76ers, finally won MVP in 2023 after being the runner-up in the previous two seasons.

49. Jayson Tatum earned a spot on the All-NBA First Team twice in 2022 and 2023, was selected for the All-NBA Third Team in 2020, named to the NBA All-Rookie First Team in 2018, and was a two-time NBA Rising Star in 2018 and 2019.

50. Robert Horry is not a Hall of Famer but has won seven NBA championships with three different teams, earning him the nickname "Big Shot Rob" for his clutch performances.

51. Kareem Abdul-Jabbar holds the record for the most MVP awards in NBA history, with six to his name.

52. LeBron James has appeared in the NBA Finals more than any other player in the modern era, with ten appearances.

53. Michael Jordan and Scottie Pippen formed one of the most successful duos in NBA history, winning six NBA championships together with the Chicago Bulls.

54. Kobe Bryant was selected to 18 All-Star games, the second-most in NBA history behind Kareem Abdul-Jabbar.

55. LeBron James holds the record for the most All-NBA selections, with a total of 19. Tim Duncan, Kobe Bryant, and Kareem Abdul-Jabbar are each tied for the second-highest number of All-NBA selections in history, with 15 each.

56. John Havlicek stole the ball! With five seconds remaining and the Celtics leading 110-109, Havlicek stole the ball from the Philadelphia 76ers in the final seconds of Game 7 of the 1965 Eastern Conference Finals. His iconic steal remains one of the most celebrated defensive plays in NBA history.

57. Wilt Chamberlain is the only player to score more than 4,000 points in a season and average more than 50 points per game, both of which he accomplished in the 1961-1962 season.

58. Bill Russell holds the record for the most rebounds in an NBA Finals game with 40.

59. Nate Archibald was the only player to lead the league in scoring and assists in the same season (1972-1973).

60. Elgin Baylor holds the record for most points in an NBA Finals game with 61 in Game 5 of the 1962 NBA Finals.

61. Magic Johnson was the first and only rookie to win the NBA Finals

MVP award.

62. Dennis Rodman, known for his fierce defensive play and rebound-ing prowess, won seven consecutive rebounding titles and five NBA championships.

63. Kevin Garnett, Paul Pierce, and Ray Allen were known as "The Big Three" and led the Boston Celtics to an NBA Championship in 2008.

64. In 2021, Russell Westbrook broke Oscar Robertson's record for most triple-doubles in a season, a record that stood for over 50 years.

65. Stephen Curry became the first player in NBA history to be named 2016 MVP by a unanimous vote.

66. Darko Miličić, a member of the Detroit Pistons, was the youngest player to win an NBA Championship in 2004. He was 18 years and 361 days old.

67. Moses Malone was a three-time NBA MVP who helped lead the 1983 Philadelphia 76ers to an NBA Championship.

68. David Robinson recorded a quadruple-double in 1994, showcasing his all-around game with 34 points, 10 rebounds, 10 assists, and 10 blocks.

69. Dominique Wilkins is one of the best dunkers in NBA history and a nine-time All-Star.

70. Jerry West is the only player to win Finals MVP from the losing team.

71. Julius Erving, also known as Dr. J, brought the modern style of play above the rim to the NBA. He was a two-time ABA Champion, before winning another championship with the NBA after the leagues merged.

72. On December 16, 2023, Jalen Brunson set new career records with 50 points and nine 3-pointers.

73. Hakeem Olajuwon is the NBA's all-time leader in blocks (3,830).

74. Charles Barkley is one of the most prolific rebounders in NBA history, despite being undersized for his position.

75. Clyde Drexler was a key member of the Portland Trail Blazers for 12 seasons and later won an NBA championship with the Houston Rockets.

76. George Gervin, known as "The Iceman", won four NBA scoring titles with his signature finger roll.

77. As of January 23, 2015, Klay Thompson holds the NBA record for the most points scored in a quarter, with 37 points in the third quarter against the Sacramento Kings.

78. Bob Pettit was the first player in NBA history to reach 20,000 career points.

79. Kevin McHale is considered one of the best power forwards in NBA history and won three championships with the Boston Celtics.

80. Willis Reed famously played through injury in Game 7 of the 1970 NBA Finals, inspiring the New York Knicks to victory.

81. As point guard for the New York Knicks, Walt "Clyde" Frazier helped lead the Knicks to their only two championships.

82. The choice of Jerry West as the model for the logo was not about West specifically but about capturing the soul of the sport and its athletes. The silhouette was taken from a photo of West dribbling the ball, and it perfectly represented the athleticism, competitiveness, and elegance of basketball. The logo effectively communicates the essence of basketball, making it one of the most iconic and recognized sports logos in the world.

Funniest Moments in the NBA

The NBA, while known for its intense competition and athletic prowess, also has its share of lighthearted and humorous moments that have entertained fans over the years. These moments, among many others, highlight the fun and human side of the NBA, reminding fans that amidst the high stakes and competition, there's always room for a good laugh.

1. Shaquille O'Neal's Free Throw Woes: Shaq's struggles at the free-throw line led to some amusing moments, including air balls and the infamous "Hack-a-Shaq" strategy.
2. Charles Barkley's Golf Swing: Not exactly an NBA moment, but Barkley's notoriously bad golf swing has been a source of laughter for NBA fans and golf enthusiasts alike.
3. Nick Young's Premature Celebration: Swaggy P celebrated a three-pointer before it actually went in, turning around and walking away, only for the shot to rim out.
4. JaVale McGee's On-Court Antics: From running back on defense while his team was still on offense to various other blooper-worthy plays, McGee has provided plenty of comedic relief.
5. Manu Ginobili Swats a Bat: During a game on Halloween night, Ginobili swatted a real bat out of mid-air with his bare hand, temporarily turning into an impromptu pest control expert.

6. Brian Scalabrine's Victory Speech: After winning the 2008 NBA Championship, Scalabrine delivered a hilarious speech where he jokingly compared himself to NBA legends, despite having a very limited role.

7. Dwight Howard's Impersonations: Howard has entertained fans and teammates alike with his spot-on impressions of other NBA players and celebrities.

8. Chris Bosh's Videobombing: Bosh became famous for his creative and often hilarious videobombs during post-game interviews.

9. Lance Stephenson Blows in LeBron's Ear: In an attempt to distract LeBron James during the playoffs, Stephenson blew in his ear, leading to a bewildered reaction.

10. Robin Lopez vs. NBA Mascots: Lopez has a faux rivalry with various NBA mascots, often engaging in pre-planned fights and humorous interactions.

11. Russell Westbrook's Wardrobe: Known for his unique fashion sense, Westbrook's post-game outfits have often been a topic of amusement.

12. Joel Embiid's Social Media Antics: Embiid has used Twitter and Instagram to troll other players, teams, and even fans with his witty and often hilarious posts.

13. Klay Thompson's Failed Dunk in China: During a promotional tour in China, Thompson attempted a 360-degree dunk and failed spectacularly, leading to widespread amusement online.

14. JR Smith's Untied Shoelaces: Smith once went through a phase where he untied opponents' shoelaces during games, earning a fine from the NBA.

15. Greg Popovich's In-Game Interviews: Known for his terse and often humorous responses, Popovich's interviews have become must-see TV.

16. LeBron James' Talcum Powder Toss: LeBron's pregame ritual of

tossing talcum powder into the air has led to some comical mishaps, including covering nearby fans and cameramen.

17. The Phoenix Suns' Gorilla Mascot's Pranks: The Suns' mascot is notorious for his pranks, including scaring players, referees, and fans.

18. Shaqtin' A Fool: This TV segment, hosted by Shaquille O'Neal, highlights humorous mistakes and moments from NBA games, becoming a fan favorite for laughs.

19. Andre Drummond's Free Throw Airball: Drummond, like Shaq, has had his struggles at the line, including a memorable airball that went viral.

20. Blake Griffin and Chris Paul's Commercials: Their humorous commercials for various brands showcased their comedic timing and chemistry off the court.

21. Rasheed Wallace's "Both Teams Played Hard": Wallace's repetitive use of this phrase during a post-game interview to avoid fines became a humorous and iconic moment.

22. James Harden's Defensive Lapses: Videos of Harden's sometimes lackadaisical defense have been compiled into humorous highlight reels.

23. Steph Curry's Mouthguard Throw: In a moment of frustration, Curry threw his mouthguard, hitting a fan, which led to a mix of apologies and laughs.

24. The Banana Boat Crew: A vacation photo of LeBron James, Chris Paul, Dwyane Wade, and Carmelo Anthony riding a banana boat became an enduring and amusing image among NBA fans.

25. Boban Marjanović is an all-around fun-loving guy. From his viral dance moves on the court to driving the Rocket's team bus or driving a go-kart backstage at the Clippers arena, his antics have resulted in some comical moments.

26. Tim Duncan was famously ejected by referee Joey Crawford for

laughing on the bench, a moment that has been both criticized and laughed at over the years.

27. Ben Simmons' Three-Pointer Celebration: When Simmons hit a rare three-pointer, both his teammates and the crowd reacted as if he'd won the game, highlighting the rarity of the event.

28. Quinn Cook Left Behind by Team Bus: After a Lakers' road win, Cook had to comment on a JR Smith's Instagram live video to remind them he was accidentally left at the arena, leading to a humorous social media moment.

29. Marc Gasol's Dance Moves: After winning the 2019 NBA Championship, Gasol's victory dance during the Toronto Raptors' parade became an instant comedic highlight, showcasing his less-than-graceful moves.

30. Shaquille O'Neal's On-Air Falls: Shaq has had his share of spills on the TNT set, including falling out of his chair and tripping over wires, leading to endless laughs from his colleagues and the audience.

31. Zion Williamson Breaks a Golf Club: An off-court moment where Williamson accidentally snapped a golf club during a swing at a team event, highlighting the NBA star's strength in a humorous context.

32. Nikola Jokić's Sombor Shuffle: Jokić's awkward yet effective one-legged fadeaway shot earned a quirky nickname and has amused fans with its unorthodox appearance but surprising effectiveness.

33. During a playoff game between the Los Angeles Clippers and the Golden State Warriors, Blake Griffin "accidentally" spilled his cup of water on a Warriors fan sitting courtside as he was looking up at the replay on the jumbotron, appearing frustrated after fouling out of the game. The incident, which many saw as a playful albeit cheeky jab, showcased Griffin's knack for blending competitive intensity with his well-known sense of humor.

34. Boban Marjanović and Tobias Harris's "Bromance": The pair's off-court friendship and humorous social media exchanges delighted fans, showcasing their playful personalities beyond basketball. And don't forget their "Tiny Hands" Goldfish commercial.

35. LeBron James' Taco Tuesday: LeBron's enthusiastic "Taco Tuesday" videos with his family became a viral sensation, showing a lighter, more playful side of the superstar.

36. Jimmy Butler's Coffee Business in the Bubble: Butler set up a coffee-selling operation inside the NBA bubble, humorously charging $20 per cup to his caffeine-deprived fellow players. Jimmy's having the last laugh, as this has led his successful coffee business called Big Face Coffee.

37. To the amusement of fans, Russell Westbrook showed off his dance moves during a game delay at the New York Knicks and Washington Wizards game in 2021.

38. Metta World Peace Thanks His Psychiatrist: After winning the NBA Championship, World Peace (then Ron Artest) gave a memorable shout-out to his psychiatrist during the post-game interview, a surprising and humorous moment.

39. Shaq vs Chuck 3 Point Contest on Inside the NBA: Shaq, with only one three-pointer in his entire NBA career, nailed his first shot and won the contest. He then celebrated with a break-dancing victory dance. The Inside the NBA team of Shaquille O'Neal, Charles Barkley, Ernie Johnson, and Kenny Smith shares incredible chemistry, and every episode is full of laughter.

Conclusion

As we conclude this exploration of basketball from its humble beginnings, its history and the players of the NBA, we reflect on a journey through time and talent that captures the essence of the sport. This book has traversed the evolution of basketball, highlighting the transformative moments and luminaries who have shaped it into the worldwide phenomenon it is today. From Dr. James Naismith's simple yet revolutionary idea, to the hardwood legends of the NBA, we've painted a picture of basketball's indelible impact on culture, society, and sportsmanship.

The stories of the NBA's iconic players have all contributed to the rich narrative of basketball. This book has not only recounted scores and statistics but has also celebrated the spirit, diversity, and unity that basketball promotes across all levels of play.

As we close this chapter on basketball's enduring legacy, let's carry forward the lessons of teamwork, perseverance, and excellence that resonate beyond the court. Whether you are a lifelong fan or new to the world of basketball, we hope this journey has inspired you with its stories of human achievement and the unifying power of sport.

If this book has rekindled your love for the game, offered new insights, or

CONCLUSION

simply entertained, we encourage you to share your experience. Please consider leaving a review on Amazon. Your feedback not only helps others discover the diverse and dynamic world of basketball but also celebrates the sport's ability to inspire dreams, foster connections, and break barriers. Let's keep the conversation going and continue to honor the game that brings us together.

Made in the USA
Monee, IL
05 January 2025

76115355R00020